We Read
PHONICS™

Whales

TREASURE BAY

Parent's Introduction

Welcome to **We Read Phonics**! This series is designed to help you assist your child in reading. Each book includes a story (which may be nonfiction), as well as some simple word games to play with your child. The games focus on the phonics skills and sight words your child will use in reading the story.

Here are some recommendations for using this book with your child:

1 Word Play

There are word games both before and after the story. Make these games fun and playful. If your child becomes bored or frustrated, play a different game or take a break.

Prize rhymes with size!

Very good!

Phonics is a method of sounding out words by blending together letter sounds. However, not all words can be "sounded out." **Sight words** are frequently used words that usually cannot be sounded out.

② Read the Story

After some word play, read the story aloud to your child—or read the story together, by reading aloud at the same time or by taking turns. As you and your child read, move your finger under the words.

Next, have your child read the entire story to you while you follow along with your finger under the words. If there is some difficulty with a word, either help your child to sound it out or wait about five seconds and then say the word.

③ Discuss and Read Again

After reading the story, talk about it with your child. Ask questions like, "What are some things that whales do?" and "What was the best part?" It will be helpful for your child to read this story to you several times. Another great way for your child to practice is by reading the book to a younger sibling, a pet, or even a stuffed animal!

> Whales can really jump high out of the water!

LEVEL **3** Level 3 introduces words with long "a" and long "i" (as in *late* and *like*), as well as the vowel combinations "ir," "er," and "ur" (as in *her, sir,* and *fur*). Other letter combinations include "qu" (as in *quick*), "sh" (as in *shine*), "th" (as in *math*), "ch" (as in *church*), and "tch" (as in *match*).

Whales

A We Read Phonics™ Book
Level 3

Text Copyright © 2010 by Treasure Bay, Inc.
Illustrations Copyright © 2010 by Judith Hunt
Use of photographs provided by Fotosearch © 2010

Reading Consultants: Bruce Johnson, M.Ed., and Dorothy Taguchi, Ph.D.

Special thanks to Doreen Gurrola of The Marine Mammal Center in Sausalito, CA
for reviewing the information in this book and to Judith Hunt for the illustrations
and information on helping to save the whales.

We Read Phonics™ is a trademark of Treasure Bay, Inc.

Published by
Treasure Bay, Inc.
P.O. Box 119
Novato, CA 94948 USA

Printed in Malaysia

Library of Congress Catalog Card Number: 2009929512

ISBN: 978-1-60115-320-3

Visit us online at:
www.TreasureBayBooks.com

P-11-17

Whales

By Leslie McGuire

Illustrations by Judith Hunt

Helping to Save the Whales
Special Information for Parents
on page 28

Phonics Game

Picture Walk

Help prepare your child to read the story by previewing pictures and words.

That's a ship!

Can you find the word ship on the page?

1. Turn to page 4. Point to the word *whale*. Ask your child to point to the whale in the picture. Read the sentence to your child.

2. Turn to page 5. Read the words, "A humpback whale is quite big." Ask your child, "What is big?" Make sure your child answers with both words: *humpback whale.* Ask your child to point to the words on the page and read those words.

3. Turn to page 6. Point to the picture. Ask your child what is in the picture. Ask more questions until your child answers *ship.* Ask your child to point to the word *ship* on the page.

4. Continue "walking" through the story, asking questions about the pictures or the words. Encourage your child to talk about the pictures and words you point out.

5. As you move through the story, you can also help your child read some of the new or more difficult words.

Sight Word Game

Go Fish

Play this game to practice sight words used in the story.

Do you have *down*?

Sorry! You'll have to go fish!

Materials:

Option 1—Fast and Easy: To print the game materials from your computer, go online to www.WeReadPhonics.com, then go to this book title and click on the link to "View & Print: Game Materials."

Option 2—Make Your Own: You'll need 18 index cards and a marker. Write each word listed on the right on two cards. You will now have two sets of cards.

1. Using one set of cards, ask your child to repeat each word after you. Shuffle both decks of cards together, and deal three cards to each player. Put the remaining cards face down in a pile.

2. Player 1 asks player 2 for a particular word. If player 2 has the word card, then he passes it to player 1. If player 2 does not have the word card, then he says, "Go fish," and player 1 takes a card from the pile. Player 2 takes a turn.

3. Whenever a player has two cards with the same word, he puts those cards down on the table and says the word out loud. The player with the most matches wins the game.

4. Keep the cards and combine them with other sight word cards you make. Use them all to play this game or play sight word games featured in other **We Read Phonics** books.

do

small

all

down

of

are

baby

for

does

This is a small whale.

A humpback whale
is quite big.

This whale is the size of a ship.

A whale can swim all the time.

It can nap when it swims!

A whale has a vent on top.

The killer whale
gulps down fish.

It can dive to hunt the fish.

Humpback whales filter water to catch krill.

Krill are like small shrimp.

A whale is a mammal,
not a fish.

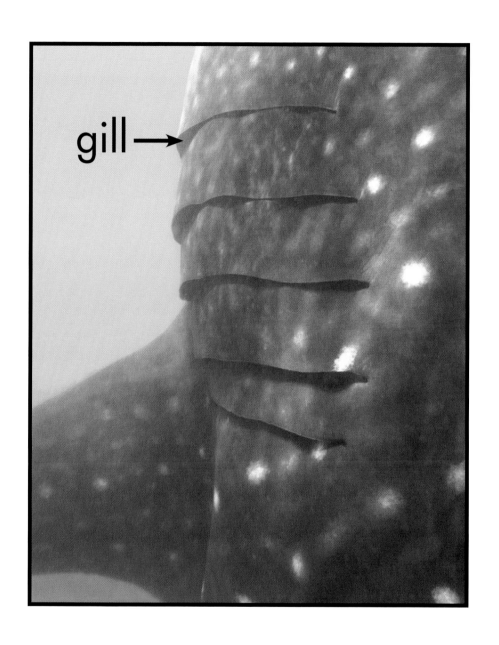

gill →

A fish has gills. A whale
does not have gills.

A baby whale drinks
thick whale milk.

A baby whale is big like a bus!

This whale jumps for fun!

A whale swims with
pals in a pod.

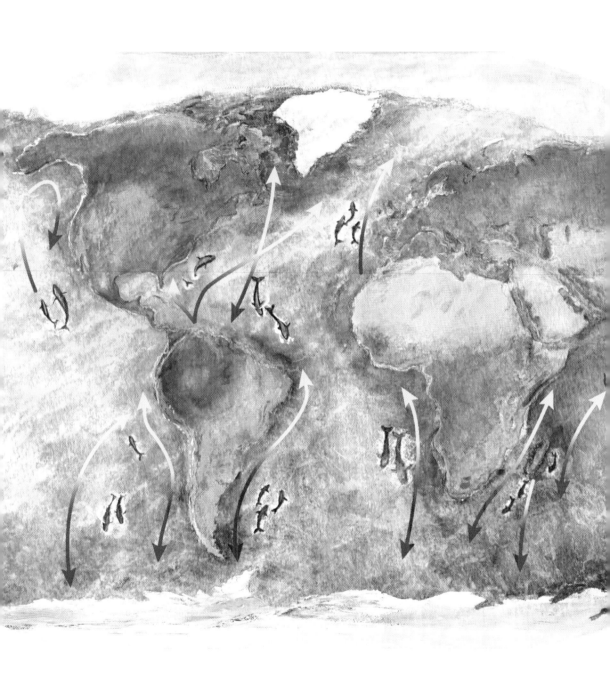

Pods can take big trips.

Whales can do a lot!

Whales can sing too!

Whales are good
for the planet.

Whales are not all safe.

We can help save
the whales.

Phonics Game

I am Thinking

Recognizing final letter sounds will help in reading new words.

Can you think of another word that ends with the sound mmmm?

Time!

1. Explain to your child that the sound "l" (make the sound for "l") ends the words *whale, krill,* and *small.*

2. Say: "I am thinking of a word from the story that ends with the sound 'l'. Can you tell me a word from the story that ends with the 'l' sound?" Possible answers include *whale, all, krill, small,* **and** *gill.*

3. If your child has trouble, offer some possible answers or repeat step 1 with different letter sounds and words.

4. When successful, repeat step 2 with these final letter sounds: d, p, k, t, g, m, s, n, v, and f.

5. For more practice, chose additional words outside of the story.

Phonics Game

Blending Sounds

Blending letter sounds together helps children learn to read new words.

A humpback wh...a...le is quite big!

1. Read this sentence to your child, but for the word *whale,* say the three sounds in the word separately: "A humpback *w..ā..l* is quite big."

2. Now ask your child, "What is quite big?" Answer: A whale.

3. If your child needs more help, try a few more examples, or try to stretch the sounds and say them closer together, as in *www-āāā-lll.*

4. Continue with the sentences below. You can also do this with other sentences from the story.
   A whale swims all the *t..ī..m.* When does a whale swim?
       Answer: All the time.
   A whale can nap when it *s..w..ĭ..m..z.* When can a whale nap?
       Answer: When it swims.
   A killer whale gulps down *f..ĭ..sh.* What does a killer whale gulp down?
       Answer: Fish.
   Humpback whales filter water to catch *k..r..ĭ..l.* What do humpback whales catch?
       Answer: Krill.
   We can *h..ĕ..l..p* save the whales. What can we do?
       Answer: Help save the whales.

Helping to Save the Whales

Special Information for Parents

There are many different kinds of whales that live in the oceans, some of them in danger of extinction. Some whales are still hunted for food and others die when they are accidentally caught in fishing nets. Global warming and noise from ships and sonar have also been identified as threats. However, one of the greatest dangers to whales is the increasing pollution of the Earth's oceans.

If you and your child would like more information about whales, and what can be done to help protect them and their ocean habitats, you can visit your local library or look online. Here are a few Web sites that you might want to check out:

www.marinemammalcenter.org

www.wwf.org.au/ourwork/oceans/whales

www.whaleadoption.org/kids.asp

www.oceanalliance.org